"A literate, comforting, thought-provoking look at some of the most magnificent "songs" of the ages, as seen through the eyes of these extraordinarily honest, contemporary women—*The Dance of Heaven* resonates with all of the emotional power and tenderness of the Psalms."

RUSS AND TORI TAFF,
RECORDING ARTISTS AND SONGWRITERS

"These women *know* the place where God meets us here on earth.... Personally, I am grateful for the courage they've had to recount the truth of God's extreme grace."

JENNIFER KNAPP,
RECORDING ARTIST AND SONGWRITER

REFLECTIONS ON PSALMS

by 21st–Century Psalmists

The

DANCE
of HEAVEN

Swept Away into the Arms of God

✜

Compiled by

BECKY SOWERS

Multnomah®Publishers *Sisters, Oregon*

THE DANCE OF HEAVEN

© 2001 by Becky Sowers
International Standard Book Number 1-57673-987-2

Cover image by John Bildbyra/Photonica
Cover design by David Carlson Design

Printed in the United States of America

For information:
Multnomah Publishers, Inc.•P.O. Box 1720•Sisters, OR 97759

Library of Congress Cataloging-in-Publication Data:

The dance of heaven : swept away into the arms of God : reflections on
Psalms by 21st-century psalmists/compiled by Becky Sowers.
    p. cm.
  ISBN 1-57673-987-2 (hardback)
  1.Bible. O.T. Psalms—meditations. I. Sowers, Becky.
  BS1430.54 .D33 2001
  242'.5—dc212001000994

01 02 03 04 05 06 07 08 — 10 9 8 7 6 5 4 3 2 1 0

C•nTents

✛

AckN•wLeDgMeNTs

I would like to thank Margaret, Nichole, Michelle, Ashley, Rebecca, Bonnie, and Kim for embracing the vision of this book and opening up their lives and innermost thoughts for the entire world to see.

I would also like to offer thanks to the wonderful supporters of this project from its infancy: Glenda McNalley, Janet Bozeman, Melissa Campbell, Jackie Russell, Christiev Carothers, and Ken Ruettgers. Thank you all for your belief in me. A very special thanks to Margaret Becker for producing the companion CD that completes this project.

Thank you also to my lifetime friends, Anne Malham and Kim Woffard. The years are adding up—thank you for your constant presence.

And to my amazing family: Mom and Dad, thanks for instilling in me a faith-based foundation upon which I have built my life. To my brothers Steve and Ken and their Traci/ys, my sweet nephew Jacob, and my exceptional (and brilliant) nephew Steven: God blessed me with a loving family. Thank you all.

F●rew●RD

BECKY SOWERS

EARLY IN MY LIFE, I developed a love for music. It wasn't a love for playing music, though my mom did attempt to get me to learn the piano (I hated the practicing part). I toyed with the idea of singing in the church choir and occasionally performing solos. But mainly, I liked to listen. I would drive around in my car to the accompaniment of Carly Simon, Dan Fogelberg, Amy Grant, Carole King, James Taylor, and John Denver. I learned every word of every song—to this day I can sing, word for word, all of these artists' lyrics! I was always convinced that in some mysterious way, these troubadours must have known exactly how I felt about life and love.

Not surprisingly, given my affection for music, I worked in radio for years, then landed at the Country Music Association. Part of my job required that I present certificates of achievement to songwriters and artists. As I got to know these amazing people—poets who put my life to music—a tremendous respect for them began to grow. My years in the music industry afforded me the privilege of literally sitting with these gifted people as they told the stories behind the crafting of their songs. I—unartistic, not musically inclined—listened in awe at the words and melodies that soared from the minds and hearts of these artists. Whenever I bought a new CD, I immediately tore open the packaging to get to the lyrics and the writers' credits.

Several years later I spent some time working within the Christian music industry. Again I found myself poring over the lyrics and feeling "songwriterstruck." I asked my new songwriting friends, "How do you do that? How do you come up with a lyric like this?" I always hoped for an answer that I could relate to, but no; as my wonderful friend Michelle Tumes once answered, "It just plopped into my head." While I know that God has showered me with other gifts, this is one that I admit being envious of: No matter how hard I try, nothing "plops" into my head. So I forge ahead, nurturing my admiration—loving the songwriters for their talents, loving God for bestowing such a life-giving gift on these people. After all, what would our world be like without music? Can you imagine the quiet, the sadness, the boredom? It's a sobering thought.

Recently I was reading the lyrics to yet another favorite song, and I thought, *These words are stunning*. I could see what the writer envisioned and feel what inspired her craftsmanship. And it struck me: *The song reads like a poem!* I checked the lyrics of other articulate artists and found my theory confirmed. Lyrics are poetry—in fact, they are modern-day psalms.

Let me explain: My Baptist upbringing afforded me the opportunity to learn much about the Bible, and I know that the ancient Psalms are considered some of the most beautiful writings of all time. And many of them were written as songs! They are wonderful works of literature just as they are God-given songs of praise, despair, joy, and sorrow.

So I began to see these contemporary artists as twenty-first-century psalmists. They write today about the same human emotions that King David wrote about. They effectively express the struggle that we as human followers of a magnificent God face in this complicated world. Hence, the idea for this book was born.

You will find here a collection of writings by women. Each of the women featured in this book has something powerful to say. Each is in a different place in life: single, engaged, newly married, married awhile, enduring a difficult divorce, or divorced.

These writings offer empathy, solace, and perspective. They illustrate that we sometimes find ourselves in less-than-perfect circumstances. Oftentimes we take a dangerous road, ignoring the signs that say, Enter at Your Own Risk or Closed to Thru Traffic. What then? Does God leave us in a heap and say, "Too bad…told you so…it was your choice"? Of course not.

He loves us through the hurt, through the uncertainty, and through the success. He draws us to the other side where we find healing, peace, and rest.

Besides offering comfort and insight from modern-day psalmists, this book has another purpose—one that is tied to another strong affection in my life: high school kids. For many years I was blessed to work with youth groups as well as with the wonderful organization Young Life. Many years ago, while I was living in Oklahoma City, a group of high school boys I knew decided to go out and party, carouse, and drink. They ended up rolling their pickup truck—four died, one lived. This tragedy inspired a recent decision on my part to leave the music business and accept a position as Tennessee's executive director for Mothers Against Drunk Driving (MADD). I firmly support actions to prevent drinking and driving, especially among the young people of today.

Alcohol is linked to the three leading causes of death—car crashes, suicides, and homicides—among those ages fifteen to twenty. Alcohol also plays a role in a majority of sexual assaults and teenage pregnancies. Unfortunately, many parents see alcohol as a lesser of evils ("At least it's not drugs") and a rite of passage ("I drank when I was a kid"). As a result, alcohol-associated problems are growing at a tremendous rate every year. Studies show that most students have experimented with alcohol by the age of twelve! It is because of this ongoing challenge that a portion of the proceeds from this book will benefit the MADD Youth in Action program of Tennessee. Youth in Action teaches high school students the skills that will effect change and discourage underage drinking within their community and state.

The Dance of Heaven is now in your hands. It is my hope that you will catch a glimpse into the hearts of these devoted women and, in doing so, further appreciate and grow to love the modern-day psalmist. It's my desire that you will open your heart to their messages and music and ask God to speak to you through their art.

By purchasing this book, you are helping to touch the hearts and minds of our young people through MADD Youth in Action. For that, I thank you.

COMING CLEAN

BONNIE KEEN

When I kept silence [before I confessed],
        my bones wasted away through my groaning
        all the day long.
For day and night [Your hand [of displeasure]
        was heavy upon me;
my moisture was turned into the drought of summer.

—Psalm 32:3–4, AMP

I RECENTLY REALIZED that in today's society, I am unmistakably politically incorrect. Why? Because I use the J-word. Though it seems rather acceptable to talk about God, I have to go and use the word *Jesus*.

The only reason I've survived my life to this point is because Jesus Christ loves messy people with messy lives and has given me the gift of forgiveness and grace to face each day. In short, God through Jesus proved that He loves sinners. *Sinners*—now that's not a word one hears often anymore. I must say that as I wrestle with the subjects of sin, confession, and forgiveness, I am aware that there are several opposing attitudes prevalent in our day and time. Approaching God for grace and absolution is, by and large, politically incorrect and viewed as an unnecessary step toward wholeness.

The fact is that we have to face the S-word *(sin)* if we are ever to accept salvation from Jesus. Free will has allowed many to choose lifestyles that leave no room for absolutes and therefore no room for sin. The notion of sin is archaic and outdated—to some, perhaps even irrelevant.

My personal definition of sin:

Sin, noun or verb: the most difficult behavior to admit, let go of, and give to God. Taking various forms for various humans, it can be summarized for most as follows:

So I've Nose-dived.

We all nose-dive in one way or another every day. Hard as we may try to avoid the free fall, we enter this world pushing through, fighting for air, and crying aloud. From there we fall down countless times, and hopefully we get up again with the will to move forward. Some of us may find it hard to believe that God almighty can love us in our sinful states. It can seem that we are perpetually nose-diving into situations not even God can stomach. Of course, there is nothing that can separate us from Him, no place so ugly that God is not present. The Word is clear on this:

If I say, Surely the darkness shall cover me
 and the night shall be [the only] light about me,
Even the darkness hides nothing from You,
 but the night shines as the day;
the darkness and the light are both alike to You.

—PSALM 139:11–12, AMP

There is much to be gained by admitting our defeats. For those people who are honest enough to expose the darkest parts of their hearts to the light of God's hands, there awaits tremendous peace and the undeserved favor called *grace*. Darkness does not frighten the Father. Darkness holds no barriers between our souls and the one who made us.

What an astounding gift I found during my own bouts with clinical depression: that God was indeed in the abyss with me. He was there in the darkest, most terrifying moments when even my will to live was on the line. In this state of desperation, I found the secret of leaning on the personality of God and the humanity and divinity of Christ. I found that forgiveness was in my grasp through the character of God.

When I could find no strength in the character of my own weak heart, I fell apart and asked for forgiveness based on what the Bible says about God. I did this in spite of how dismal my circumstances appeared (I was a single mother of two, divorced, and full of failure). Oh, that we all can remember to pray with increasing passion and full comprehension the words of the psalmist:

Blessed [happy, fortunate, to be envied] is he
        who has forgiveness of his transgression
continually exercised upon him,
        whose sin is covered.
For this [forgiveness] let everyone who is godly pray—
        pray to You in a time when You may be found;
surely when the great waters [of trial] overflow,
        they shall not reach [the spirit in] him.

—PSALM 32:1, 6, AMP

Our sins are covered and even forgotten. For those of us who fear the next pratfall into sin—especially when we are trying to gain new ground after divorce, depression, loss, betrayal, financial devastation—let us stand on the Word of God and not on ourselves. He promises that when great trials flood the banks of our lives, He will protect the spirit within us. There is nothing to fear—except that we might not take our pain to God for absolution and healing. *Lord, may our knees never be too stiff to bow before You for deliverance and forgiveness in every season of our pain and journey!*

On any given day, stiff knees may not be our problem. Perhaps it is a prideful inclination to avoid the S-word altogether. This attitude is apparent even in some church circles. I wonder if, in an effort to have "people-friendly" churches, we have held back the great gift of admitting to sin, thus denying others the joy of God's forgiveness. Hoping to attract the masses and hesitant to offend, have we sidetracked the beauteous splendor of falling on our faces before the Lord with repentant, broken hearts?

Ponder this statement: *Maybe I'm wrong.* These are three of the hardest words for mortals to spit out. *I'm sorry* comes even closer to admitting sin and looms as another of the most difficult phrases to utter. But the phrase *I've sinned* sounds just ridiculous! Nobody *sins* here in the Western Hemisphere. Instead, one *moves on.* One *evolves.* One *deepens* spiritually and intellectually in order to gain enlightenment. We consume the lie that we can take care of our failures on our own terms.

Consider this verse:

I acknowledged my sin to You,
    and my iniquity I did not hide.
I said, I will confess my transgressions to the Lord
[continually unfolding the past till all is told]—
    then You [instantly] forgave me the guilt and
iniquity of my sin.

—PSALM 32:5, AMP

Yet as wondrous and healing as forgiveness is, I know it's hard to accept such bounty. I was raised in an environment that emphasized judgment not forgiveness, and estrangement not reconciliation. Theologically speaking, I was taught a great deal about the Bible and God and Jesus. They were years of stellar church attendance—three times a week and vacation Bible school—and studies on how every denomination was wrong but ours. At age twelve I was baptized, mostly out of fear, as I was taught that at that age all of my sins began to "count."

Somewhere in the middle of all this, God was faithful beyond measure to woo my heart to know Him. Many years and unforgettable seasons of pain later I experienced the astounding presence of His touch, mercy, grace, and forgiveness. The closer I came to the reality of Christ's love for hurting people, the more my own sins came to light. The more I learned of the price Christ paid for my forgiveness, the more I was led to seek that forgiveness like water for my thirsty heart. This mercy I received began to grow in me a slowly embraced desire to forgive others!

Everything is gained by admitting aloud our need for forgiveness and then making a childlike acceptance of God's great love. I finally took what I call the "bungee jump of faith" into the arms of God. And what freedom I found in that free fall! I discovered the glory of my weakness, the release of torment in admitting my humanity without qualification. Brokenness—without the paralysis of analysis—became a friend. The key to this freedom and release was simply the repentant utterance before God the Father, "Forgive me, for I have sinned. I am a sinner saved by the right hand of my God and the blood of Jesus. I cannot earn this staggering gift, nor will I ever deserve it. I can accept it with humility and joy."

Or, as Mozart wrote, "Remember, merciful Jesus, that I am the cause of your journey."

You are a hiding place for me;
*   You, Lord, preserve me from trouble.*
You surround me with songs and shouts of deliverance.

—PSALM 32:7, AMP

In August 1996, I was studying King David's life, and I came upon the events that unfold in 2 Samuel 11–12. David had chosen to have an affair with Bathsheba and to murder her husband. These were devastating decisions he made even after years of precious intimacy with God the Father, years in which he experienced such powerful instances as slaying a giant and seeing God's hand move mightily in raising him to be king of Israel. How could David, this man so in tune with God's own heart, be capable of inflicting such pain on himself and others with these Technicolor sins? Didn't his sin prove that he was a wretched mess? Didn't his abysmal failures negate the pious tone of the Twenty-third Psalm?

As I was reading, I studied with new eyes the account of David's reaction to the death of his infant child—the first child conceived with Bathsheba. He cried out to God, begged for mercy for his sick child's life, refused to eat or sleep for days…and then the child died anyway. So what did David do? Blame God? Blame himself? Bury himself in ashes of shame? Sink into despair?

No. To my utter amazement (and evidently those around him at the time), David got up, took a bath, ate, and went in to the comforting arms of Bathsheba. It was on that very night that Solomon was conceived!

When asked about this abrupt turnaround of attitude, David replied that he had asked God to help his son. He prayed from a lifestyle of trust in God's faithfulness with all of his might. And then he accepted God's verdict. This kind of trust demands intense time with God and faith in what God sees that we cannot.

David knew beyond words and weeping and shouting and doubt that his God was to be trusted. He put his full passion and weight and faith in the character of God and in God's forgiveness. In that knowledge, David found peace and deliverance from the voices in his own head. Thus he could write:

Many are the sorrows of the wicked,
but he who trusts in, relies on, and confidently leans
on the Lord shall be compassed about
with mercy and with loving-kindness.

—PSALM 32:10, AMP

David's trust in God came from knowing God. David had learned, through experience, that God was merciful beyond understanding. He had an ongoing, passionate, inquisitive, demanding, tearful, and ultimately submissive relationship with the God of his fathers, his heritage, and his future. God honored this relationship by bringing His own Son to earth through David's lineage. Unthinkable! Incomprehensible mercy!

Now when I read Psalm 51, which David penned after confessing his sin with Bathsheba, I choke up. Sometimes tears fall as I long for this kind of intimacy with God. I want the kind of trust that led David to pray:

> Have mercy on me O God,
>   according to Your steadfast love;
> according to the multitude of
>   Your tender mercy and loving-kindness
> blot out my transgressions.
>   Wash me thoroughly [and repeatedly]
> from my iniquity and guilt and cleanse me
>   and make me wholly pure from my sin!
> For I am conscious of my transgressions
>   and I acknowledge them;

my sin is ever before me.
     Against You, You only, have I sinned
and done that which is evil in Your sight,
     so that You are justified in your sentence
and faultless in Your judgment.

—PSALM 51:1–4, AMP

As I read on in Psalm 51, I realize that the most unspeakable joy I can have is in knowing that God honors this kind of brokenness. All the ill I have done and may still do in my life is first and foremost a grievance I have committed against my Father God. And before Him I must take my case and lay down my woundedness. Then He is not slow to respond. His forgiveness is immediate, whether I have the good sense to receive it or not.

What I find, sooner or later, is mercy, forgiveness, grace, and a truly renewed spirit. It's almost too simple a miracle to let into my being. Yet that is the only way to accept such an enormous gift: With sweaty, worn, undeserving palms, I reach out to receive the outpouring of God's love in His forgiveness and mercy. It runs over me like longed-for rain on dry, parched soil.

Make me to hear joy and gladness and be satisfied;
let the bones which You have broken rejoice.
Hide Your face from my sins and blot out
all my guilt and iniquities.
Create in me a clean heart, O God,
and renew a right, persevering,
and steadfast spirit within me.
Cast me not away from Your presence
and take not Your Holy Spirit from me.
Restore to me the joy of Your salvation
and uphold me with a willing spirit.

—PSALM 51:8–12, AMP

And a final thought on the S-word: God's response—this kind of scandalous, ridiculous, otherworldly forgiveness given so freely to me—demands that I extend this grace to others. It would be insane for me to believe that I could be so sweetly and completely absolved without being moved to give this gift as often as possible to those who have sinned against me. Forgiveness wipes away bitterness. Forgiveness opens the door for second chances. Forgiveness is medicine for the soul.

David, the psalmist and lover of God's heart, said so:

Then will I teach transgressors Your ways,
　　and sinners shall be converted and return to You.
Deliver me from bloodguiltiness and death, O God,
　　the God of my salvation, and my tongue shall sing
aloud of Your righteousness
　　(Your rightness and Your justice).
For You delight not in sacrifice, or else I would give it;
　　You find no pleasure in burnt offering.
My sacrifice [the sacrifice acceptable]
　　to God is a broken spirit; a broken
and a contrite heart
　　[broken down with sorrow for sin and humbly and
thoroughly penitent],
　　such, O God, You will not despise.

—PSALM 51:13–14; 16–17, AMP

Lord, I pray for all of us the ability

to fall down before You

and speak aloud the deepest secrets

that You already know exist.

May we turn to You alone and

not to any substitute of our culture

to find mercy and forgiveness for our sins.

Let us admit that we have broken Your heart

and that we must be healed by asking Your forgiveness first.

Then in the spirit of Your servant David

may we rest in the great,

unthinkable, undeserved favor of Your heart's character

for complete and total absolution of our sins.

As you have promised to forgive,

may we accept this benevolence

and neither wander nor wallow

in the condemnation of our past.

Help us, dear Father, precious Christ,

and tender Holy Spirit,

to move on in our lives,

having been forgiven and made clean,

to reach out to others and extend this arm

of Your grace to those around us.

In our own little corners of the world,

may we find in You the strength

to love and breathe into this world,

through the breath of our lives,

the gift to others of Your great mercy.

In Christ's most holy name,

and alleluia through His blood,

amen.

A SONG OF REPENTANCE

Sweet Forgiveness

There is no shame for the heart that is broken
New life I stand to gain in You by laying down despair
There is no blame, no condemnation
God delights in every honest prayer
O sweet forgiveness

Fall on me
Forgive me Lord, it's You alone that I grieve
Amazing mercy is what I need
Cleanse me Lord, it's You alone who know me
O sweet forgiveness
Sweet forgiveness

Fall on me
For every tear I have brought into Your eyes
Each time I drove another nail into the hands of Christ
For every chance for repentance I let slip by
Lord forgive me, hear my every cry
O sweet forgiveness

Fall on me
Forgive me Lord, it's You alone that I grieve
Amazing mercy is what I need
Cleanse me Lord, it's You alone who know me
O sweet forgiveness
Sweet forgiveness
Fall on me

Create a new and right spirit in my soul
O God of grace, now make me whole

O sweet forgiveness
Fall on me
Forgive me Lord, it's You alone that I grieve
Amazing mercy is what I need
Cleanse me Lord, it's You alone who know me
O sweet forgiveness
Sweet forgiveness
Fall on me

SıGHs & LᴏNGıNGs

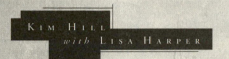

KıM HıLL
with LıSA HARPER

O God, you are my God,

earnestly I seek you;

my soul thirsts for you,

in a dry and weary land

where there is no water.

—PSALM 63:1

November 2000: I just came home from running errands, and the baby-sitter told me that my seven-year-old son, Graham, had asked her if I was out on a date. He told her that he'd watched a Disney program about a boy his age whose parents divorced, and the movie dealt with the boy's conflicted feelings about his mother's reentry into the dating scene. I never thought I'd have to sit on my little boy's bed and assure him that unlike the mom in the movie, I wasn't dating anyone.

It's been only a few days since I had to explain to him that I can't be with him and his brother this Thanksgiving. That was the hardest thing I've ever had to tell my brave first-grader. His little brother, my blond and boisterous three-year-old, Benjamin, isn't asking as many questions as Graham is. But his little heart has obviously been buffeted by the waves of tension and chaos that rolled through our house as consistently as any ocean.

Their daddy has been gone for two months now. But instead of abandonment, I feel relief. Abandonment was what I experienced alone in the hospital the night before Benjamin was born. Then, I longed for a loving husband to stay with me while I anxiously listened to beeps as machines monitored the baby's and my blood pressure. Now, I long mostly for peace and stability. And our home finally feels peaceful—most days, anyway. The boys and I have been baking cookies, singing songs, and literally sighing with contentment.

But sometimes, after I supervise their bathroom routines, help with pajamas, read stories, say good-night prayers, and walk downstairs, I sigh again. The storms of unrest have taken their toll on the shores of my soul, too. Nine years of marriage have left me feeling ninety years old. I'm tired and disillusioned and bruised. Some days I long to be loved well, and some days I just long to be alone.

Lord, I come to You for safety.
Please hear my cry and come to save me.
Rescue me.
Be my mighty rock.

You are so faithful to me—
I trust You, Lord.
You see my troubles, You care about me.

I trust You, my life is in Your hands.
Please save me from those who want to hurt me.

I know if I call out to You
You won't let me down.

I felt like I was separated from You
That You didn't see me;
But You heard me when I cried out for help.

You answered me.
Be strong—trust in Me with all your heart, Kim.
Hope in Me.

(MY INTERPRETATION OF PSALM 31)

Recently, a well-meaning pastor told me that he wished I'd given God time to heal our marriage and my estranged husband. It was all I could do not to scream. It's not like we had a good marriage and just recently hit a little bump on Matrimonial Bliss Boulevard. Since the second week of our marriage, I have felt as if I am hurtling through life on a roller coaster. I just can't hang on any longer. My urge for defensive posturing was soon replaced by an overwhelming desire to curl up into a ball and sob. It doesn't seem like anyone really understands the turmoil of the last decade. I guess I hid it too well.

For a long time I thought that if I was completely honest about the devastation in our marriage, God's reputation might be harmed. I was afraid that if I couldn't make my marriage work, I'd wear a scarlet letter for the rest of my life, that nothing else I ever did would be good enough to reconcile such a massive mistake. I saw divorce as the unpardonable sin and really didn't think God's grace would visit that dark corner of my world. If I just prayed a little harder, served a little more selflessly, and expected a little less, eventually my penance would pay off in a healthy marriage. It wouldn't be perfect, mind you, but bearable. I was determined not to be another failed marriage statistic, so I hung on for dear life. Letting go was the most difficult decision I've ever made.

[Journal entry] I'm so tired of being hurt every day. I know that only the Lord will not disappoint me. He is always faithful—will always hold me, will always listen to me. Lord, please help me. I don't want to give up…please rescue me. You are my rock. Lord, be my shield. I put my trust in You: "Great peace have those who love Your law / And nothing causes them to stumble. Let Your hand become my help, / For I have chosen Your precepts" (Psalm 119:165, 173, NKJV).

One day, when I was at the very end of my frayed rope, I had a conversation with a dear friend's husband, who asked me this question: "Kim, can you just tell the Lord that you will endure with Him regardless of what happens in your marriage?"

His question stung me. Until that moment I hadn't realized that I was mad at God. I knew I was mad at Rob. And I could justify that anger. But Joe's question exposed the real struggle in my soul—my anger at God for asking me to trust Him no matter what my circumstances were.

I went home that night, his question still ringing in my ears, and sat in the bathtub and sobbed. I cried for so long that my toes and fingers shriveled like little prunes—which was pretty much what my heart felt like. At one point, I literally said out loud to God, "Okay, I will trust You!" And it's at that moment that I felt the heaviness in my spirit lift.

I wish I could find the words to better explain what took place in the tub, because something tangible happened, and I didn't feel quite so hopeless. I knew more than ever before that I could trust Him completely with my deepest longings and disappointments.

[Journal entry] O Lord, I continue to be amazed at how You come and rescue me when I am drowning. I have cried out to You, but not enough. Yet You hear the prayers of those who are interceding on my behalf.

I am undone. I am truly humbled. Wherever I turn, You are there. This morning I recognized Your counsel in the voice on the radio in the car. You are speaking to me in any way You can. I heard Your voice this morning as I awoke: "Trust Me, Kim. I will never leave you nor forsake you."

Of course, my bathroom breakthrough wasn't a one-time cure-all. I continue to have days when hope is elusive and peace is fleeting. I still have more questions than answers. Why did God allow me to marry this man if He knew the disastrous path that lay ahead? Why didn't He intervene? What's wrong with me that would cause me to make such a poor decision? If I missed God's voice then, will I hear Him clearly now? I struggle to reach the bowls on the top kitchen shelves that Rob used to get for me, and I wonder if my questions are reaching the omniscience of God in the highest heavens.

So many times I wish I could escape,
To fly away like a bird
To hide in the wilderness—
It's not an enemy who hates me;
I think I could deal with that.
But it's the one I have loved and trusted
Who has betrayed me.
You tell me to throw my burdens down at Your feet,
That You will carry them and carry me.
That You won't allow those who live right to fall—
But I still feel as if I'm falling apart,

Please hold me up.
I trust You, Lord.

(MY INTERPRETATION OF PSALM 55)

I confess that I'm having a hard time dealing with the fact that I won't be with my boys for Thanksgiving. In an attempt for a peaceful settlement, I've agreed to let Rob have Graham and Benjamin every other weekend and most of the holidays this year. I keep telling myself that I get to be with them every day. I get to see Graham's grin each afternoon when he runs to the car with his bulging backpack. And I get my very own wake-up call every morning—"Get up, Mama, it's mornin' time!"—courtesy of precious early-bird Benjamin.

But I still can't imagine Thanksgiving without my boys. They love to play games and put on elaborate plays with their cousins for all the grown-ups. Graham was so excited because he had learned to play a few songs on his little keyboard and had memorized Psalm 100 especially for the holiday entertainment extravaganza. Benjamin was excited, too, mostly about getting to be with his "very best friend, Gus" (my sister Lacey's son, who's just a week older than Benjamin). He's too little to understand why he has to be with his "other" cousins.

[Journal entry] Father, I pray for Your peace…for You to surround all of us. Cover Graham and Benjamin with Your mercy and protection. Guard their little hearts and minds, O Lord…protect them. Give me Your wisdom with them and through all of this. Please give me the right words to say to both of them. Heal them—make them whole. I know that You are able to weave together even what is terrible into good…be their perfect Father…be their best friend, Jesus. Make up for what they are missing. Be my peace so that I can be stable for them. You are the strength of my life. You are my defender and deliverer. I am holding on to You. I am putting all of my trust in You. I will not fear what man can do to me…You are my protector, my husband, my Father, the lover of my soul…my all in all.

December 2000: Thanksgiving has come and gone. It was harder than I can express to pack the boys' duffel bags and watch them walk down the front steps and climb into the car with their dad. I wanted to hold on forever when I hugged them good-bye; but I let go long before I wanted to so they wouldn't see me crying. Yet God continues to be my rock. He really is my strength when I am weak.

In the midst of my loneliness without Graham and Benji, God provided constant reminders of His presence, such as...unexpected snow covering the ground with a blanket of sparkling white...a rental-car fiasco that turned into a pleasant experience (no less than a modern miracle!)...a perfect pumpkin bisque that I didn't have to cook...the laughter of good friends...and most of all, my sons' happy voices on the phone assuring me they were okay. They were well guarded and protected. Their heavenly Father is faithful even when their mom's faith falters.

To borrow a phrase from a wordsmith much more gifted than me, it has been "the best of times and the worst of times." I still wince from the wounds of our failed marriage, and the boys still wonder out loud if their daddy and I will be together again. But I've discovered that in my deepest sorrows, God's nearness is the sweetest. And the balm of Gilead feels most soothing on the darkest bruises of my soul. I'm learning to trust in Him who holds "happily ever after" in the palm of His hand.

Only God gives inward peace,
      and I depend on him.
God alone is the mighty rock
      that keeps me safe,
and he is the fortress
      where I feel secure.
God saves me and honors me.
      He is that mighty rock
where I find safety.
      Trust God, my friends,
and always tell him
      each one of your concerns.
God is our place of safety.

—PSALM 62:5–8, CEV

A Song of Longing

Longing for You
Your love overwhelms me
Your peace is beyond compare
Your mercy just waits to surround me
If I dare
So I kneel before You, Father
In the shadow of Your might
And I cry for You
To heal my heart tonight

O God
I'm desperate for You
Don't hide Your face from me
I need Your love to find me here

O God
I'm longing for You
Breathe Your life into my soul
Only You sustain me
Only You can make me whole

I know You in sorrow
I see You through every tear

I feel the touch of Your refining fire
When You draw near
May the scars I bear be sacred
And this brokenness be real
So these wounds
Reflect Your glory as they heal

O God
I'm desperate for You
Don't hide Your face from me
I need Your love to find me here

O God
I'm longing for You
Breathe Your life into my soul
Only You sustain me
Only You can make me whole

Strengthen me according to Your promise
Renew me with the fragrance of Your Word
Hold me up when the waters overtake me
That I may live to bring You praise

cOMFoRT IN HIS NeArNESS

MICHELLE TUMES

O Lord, I have so many enemies;
  so many are against me.
So many are saying,
  "God will never rescue him!"
But you, O Lord, are a shield around me,
  my glory, and the one who lifts my head high.
I cried out to the Lord,
  and he answered me from his holy mountain.

—PSALM 3:1–4, NLT

*C*OMFORT IS SOMETHING we all desire. I think of it as a place where we belong, where we feel safe; a place where we are protected from the distracting voices and circumstances that constantly surround us.

Sometimes we long for comfort when we feel totally alone or alienated. I grew up in a Christian family, for which I am grateful. When I was a teenager, however, the Christian way of life was not a popular one in rural South Australia. Jeered at and teased, I fought back tears and built a tough exterior. Being different was not socially acceptable, so for a while I was an outcast.

Fortunately, my parents gave me a horse, and every night after school I went riding. Sometimes I would ramble over golden fields, and other times I would gallop through vineyards, seeing only streaks of green beneath the brilliant sky. God really met me in this time of loneliness. While I was alone with Him, I felt that I belonged to the Lord. I drew spiritual strength from realizing that I did not need the acceptance of my peers—the acceptance of the Lord was more than enough. Through those riding sessions during which I fellowshiped with my God, I came to understand that wherever I was, He was walking beside me, carrying my heavy heart when I felt abandoned. His Word says, "Why am I discouraged? Why so sad? I will put my hope in God! I will praise him again—my Savior and my God!" (Psalm 42:11, NLT).

I believe that God has given us many gifts to remind us we are resting safely in the palm of His hand. Horseback riding was one gift; music is another. Writing and recording this incredible manifestation of God's peace and love bring me to a place where doubts and questions fade rapidly into insignificance. Fear itself seems to tremble in its boots, and I feel indescribable warmth. We all have those songs in our hearts that transport us to a world of wholeness and a land that seems so heavenly. When I sing, my soul overflows with joy. I know this is the Lord gently expressing His love and compassion.

One of my favorite songs is from Brahms's *Requiem,* the lyrics of which come directly from the Psalms. I sang this in high school, and when I hear it, I am reduced to tears yet elevated into the arms of my heavenly Father. I especially love the words from Psalm 84:

How lovely is your dwelling place,
    O Lord Almighty.
I long, yes, I faint with longing
    to enter the courts of the Lord.
With my whole being, body and soul,
    I will shout joyfully to the living God.

—PSALM 84:1–2, NLT

Sometimes, I admit, I feel as though my pain is so deep that I cannot be consoled. I don't understand a particular loss or the experience of rejection. Moving to Nashville from Australia a few years ago was exciting for me—I was writing songs and trying to get a record deal and making many new friends. Romance was not really on my mind, but I met a man while singing at a singles group in Hendersonville. A relationship blossomed, and I was floating on cloud nine. Everywhere I went reminded me of the new love I had found. Even as a friend and I were traveling through the south of France, I was constantly looking for a phone booth to make contact with my boyfriend in Tennessee.

My friends and family will tell you that I was besotted, smitten, and overwhelmed. Unfortunately, the dating relationship came to an abrupt halt. All the hopes and dreams I had were crushed along with my spirit. For a time I was unable to let go of the situation and move on. My idealism and optimism turned into apathy and cynicism. I had relied on a relationship, and when that was taken away, my focus was on a dark, empty void. It took a long time to see that God would never leave me or forsake me.

A Bible study was the beginning of the healing process. A group of wonderful women slowly taught me how to live in God's presence. Whenever a bad situation arose, I learned how to look to Jesus instead of to a human for rescue. The comfort of the Holy Spirit mentioned in the book of John became a reality: "I will not abandon you as orphans—I will come to you" (John 14:18, NLT). The warmth of His presence throughout my ordeal confirmed that the Lord was sitting beside me and was weeping when I wept.

For me, God sent my dear friends each Wednesday night to show His forgiveness and love. He used my mistake to draw me closer to the true Comforter.

Those who live in the shelter of the Most High
will find rest in the shadow of the Almighty....
For he orders his angels
to protect you wherever you go.
They will hold you with their hands.

—PSALM 91:1, 11–12, NLT

There are accounts from every age that suggest that God sends angels to comfort His people. Possibly the most famous is the time when Jesus was sweating drops of blood in the Garden of Gethsemane. He was preparing to be crucified. I can't even begin to imagine the anguish He was enduring. But then an angel of the Lord was sent to be with Him (Luke 22:43).

I believe angels still come to comfort us today. As a young girl, I was terribly afraid of the dark. The shadows dancing in the moonlight outside always represented intruders that were going to abduct me. My parents probably remember the many nights that I slept beside their bed.

One particular evening I heard a loud fluttering noise. I am positive that God allowed my ears to hear the fluttering of angels' wings. His emissaries protect and comfort us in fearful times.

My dad tells the story of when he was driving from the city to the outback before he was married. His little Volkswagen was hurtling along the road when a car came directly toward him at a tremendous speed. He remembers a strong force moving the steering wheel to take his vehicle out of harm's way. He attributes this to an angel guiding the car to safety. I am confident that angels protect us even though we don't see them with our mortal eyes.

For the Lord God is our light and our protector.
He gives us grace and glory.
No good thing will the Lord withhold
from those who do what is right.

—PSALM 84:11, NLT

God also presents to us the gift of His people to come alongside us when we are sad. Did you realize that the word *comfortable* is comprised of the two words *comfort* and *able?* I feel so comfortable talking to my best friend, Tina, who lives in Australia. She always offers the most rational advice—it both comforts me and makes me able to endure whatever problem I am facing.

In December of 1999, I married a wonderful man in Australia, Doug. He is another best friend. The mistake of my past relationship highlighted the beauty and mystery of this relationship that God has ordained. My husband encourages my walk with the Lord, and hand-in-hand we are growing closer to Him because He has given us each other.

There are times when the business side of my music becomes a little unsettling. My focus can wander away from what is really important. My husband is very quick to point out that trust in God is the only decision that can bring about peace and a sense of direction. His comforting advice helps me let little worries disintegrate.

Protection is a subject I often think of when comfort comes to mind. The simple fact that our lives are completely in the hands of the One who knit our chromosomes together before birth should put a few things into perspective. But I am the first to admit that whenever there is the slightest inkling of danger, adrenaline rushes through my body and I break into a cold sweat. This is something that has taught me (again) to rely on God. Whenever I fly and turbulence hits suddenly, I imagine that Jesus is the pilot! This gives me peace of mind. The flights to and from Australia are extremely time-consuming (about fourteen hours), so fretting for the entire journey is a waste of energy.

Anyone who has attended a concert knows that there are always illuminated exit signs. I am the type of person that studies them before a concert begins to make absolutely sure that everyone can escape in the event of a fire. Microphones with cords also pose questions of safety before I use them on stage—I am afraid of being electrocuted. Joey, a bass player, and I were talking one time when we were on tour. A snowstorm was forecasted for that evening, and the tour bus was headed straight into bad weather en route to our next performance. Of course, I was concerned about black ice and snow on the road. Joey said, "Just imagine how concerned you are; God cares about your safety much more than you do." That did it. I realized that God's love envelops me so much that it acts as a protective shield from harm in many circumstances.

As a child, when I was scared of the dark, I ran into my parents' bedroom. As soon as my little feet entered the room, I felt secure in the protective love of my mother and father. No harm would come to me. It is the same with my heavenly Father. Once I reach out to Him, I feel comforted and protected. God wants us to run into His presence, where there is warmth that penetrates deeper than the finest balm.

The Lord is my shepherd;
    I shall not want.
He maketh me to lie down in green pastures;
    he leadeth me beside the still waters.
He restoreth my soul:
    he leadeth me in the paths of righteousness
for his name's sake.
Surely goodness and mercy shall follow me
    all the days of my life:
and I will dwell in the house of the Lord for ever.

—PSALM 23:1–3, 6, KJV

Perhaps the most profound example of God's comfort is found in this Psalm. One day, my husband and I experienced the deep truth of the Psalm when we went to visit our priest. We were having some business problems, so we went to see Father Michael's brand-new golden retriever puppies to cheer ourselves up. There we were, holding these new, beautiful creatures, so young that some of them still hadn't opened their eyes. Father Michael spoke softly and peacefully to us. He didn't tell us that the circumstances would change immediately. Instead, he highlighted the fact that whatever situation we were in, God was offering the comfort of His "green pastures."

Sometimes it appears as though the whole world is about to destroy my sanity and security. But God will always take me to a spiritual place of protection, peace, and comfort, a place where I can lay my weary mind and open my sometimes cold and hardened heart. "Surely goodness and mercy shall follow me all the days of my life" is a promise that helps me in times of confusion and doubt. I know I will dwell within the hallowed walls of the Lord's house, which I believe is the loving will of God.

This life takes many twists and turns. None of us knows what is about to happen on this blessed and sometimes perilous journey. One thing I know is that God has promised His comfort despite my fluctuating spiritual, emotional, and physical climates. I continue to rest in my God, who scoops me up into His arms like a little child. I hope that you will be able to sense His abiding nature wherever this wonderful journey takes you.

A SONG OF COMFORT

Lovely

You're the sweet dreams that soothe me
When I can't fall asleep
You're the field in the middle of the city
When I'm rushing by at the speed of light

You're the strong resolution when I find no peace
You're the church bells ringing in the evening
When all is quiet
You whisper comfort
That lifts my heart
I get so weak

You're lovely, lovely
You're the center of my universe
A thousand times I look
Around me and I find
You're lovely, lovely
You're the center of my universe
A million ways could not explain
You're lovely

You're the soft words that touch me
When I just can't speak
You're the breeze on the ocean in the morning
Reminding me to greet the day

You're the flowers I remember seeing in Italy
Colors through a golden haze
Bright and radiant, soft and fragrant
In the noonday sun, it makes me sing

I understand there may be grief and there may be pain
But I'm aware You blind the darkness with who You are because...

You're lovely, lovely
You're the center of my universe
A thousand times I look around me and I find
You're lovely

H●PE RETURNeD

ASHLEY CLEVELAND

There are many who say,
"Who will show us any good?"
Lord, lift up the light of Your countenance upon us.
You have put gladness in my heart,
More than in the season that their grain
and wine increased.

—PSALM 4:6–7, NKJV

As far back as I can remember I have been a believer in Jesus, and even in the worst of times, I clung to the thought that God was for me. But my understanding of His nature was fairly merciless; I imagined Him carrying an ever-present measuring stick that doubled as a rod of reproof.

I'm aware today that, as the eldest child in a troubled Southern family operating under a cloud of alcoholism and critically devoted to performance and presentation, it would have been unlikely for me to think otherwise. I will probably be an overachiever all the way to the grave, but at one critical point in my life, my overachieving was all about extreme failure and a sickness that was trying to kill me.

I am feeble and severely broken;
I groan because of the turmoil of my heart.

—Psalm 38:8, NKJV

Oddly enough, the beginning of my transformation came long before there was any evidence of it in my life. It surrounded my pregnancy, which I viewed as the all-time low in a decade of lows because I was unmarried and an active addict. I was unaware of the various avenues of help that were available to me and unwilling to find out about them—I had wholeheartedly bought into the delusion that I could control my "problem" if I wanted to badly enough. My pregnancy was an exercise in white-knuckling with horrible slips that left me filled with shame, remorse, and fear over the condition of my baby. I was convinced that if God had been annoyed before, He was really mad now, and I fully expected His wrath to consume me.

In the midst of this, someone saw fit to quote Scriptures to me such as Luke 17:2, which says it would be better to get thrown into the ocean with a millstone hung around your neck than to hurt a little one. This made my terror complete, and I was sure that, one way or another, God would destroy me. But that is not what happened.

I had hidden a little picture in my heart of the child that I would hope for—if I dared to hope—and out she popped on September 14, 1982, perfect in every way. For the first time in my life I felt the Lord part the curtain between us, lean down, and whisper in my ear, "See, I'm not who you think I am."

This came as amazing news to a bewildered, broken girl, and I knew that the God I had met was tenderhearted, merciful, and personal. From that moment I dared to hope, and it was that smudge of hope that brought us to the Guitar Town.

I came to Nashville, Tennessee, in 1984, hoping to find a record deal and needing to find a life. I was a single parent with a two-year-old daughter;

despite my revelatory encounter with God, I was still entrenched in alcoholism and drug addiction. I had a natural gift for music, which kept me going with tiny flickers of hope that maybe I could become a rock star, and I had a powerful desire to survive for the sake of my child. Beyond that, very little of this move was thought out.

I arrived in Nashville knowing one college friend and one contact for possible work singing radio jingles. The contact didn't pan out, but my friend, a country singer named Pam Tillis, with whom I had spent the better part of my time at the University of Tennessee playing in clubs as a folk duo, offered me a place to live. Through Pam and various writers' nights around town I was able to begin meeting people in the music industry. Of course, I soon realized that Nashville was not a rock-and-roll town. My entire experience with country music had consisted of three records, yet I had a strong sense from the moment I entered the city limits that I was home.

Shortly after the move and during a family visit over the holidays, my mother and my sister Windsor, acting as my angels, convinced me to go to a long-term treatment facility, and I began inching my way toward recovery.

He sent from above, He took me;
  He drew me out of many waters.
He delivered me from my strong enemy,

from those who hated me,
for they were too strong for me.
He also brought me out into a broad place;
He delivered me because He delighted in me.

—PSALM 18:16–17, 19, NKJV

Over the next few years, I managed to establish a musical career as a singer, songwriter, and performer; in 1990, all of these culminated in a record deal with Atlantic Records in New York. Although by this time many things in my life had changed (some dramatically), one was still a constant: I had an undeniable talent for finding unavailable, unstable men and diving into relationships with them.

I waited patiently for the Lord;
And He inclined to me,
And heard my cry.
He also brought me up out of a horrible pit,
Out of the miry clay,
And set my feet upon a rock,
And established my steps.

—PSALM 40:1–2, NKJV

King David may have waited patiently for the Lord, but I didn't. I was single and upset about it. But all the years of taking matters into my own hands had paid off, well, nothing. My parents divorced when I was in kindergarten; their last argument was triggered by some mischief I had gotten into, and my father left for good. Trust did not figure largely into my childhood, and I knew nothing of true intimacy, especially where men were concerned.

Once I started dating, the average shelf life of my relationships was around two weeks. When I moved to Nashville, I began to make some good friendships with men, but my romantic entanglements were a mess and ultimately led nowhere. I kept choosing men who clearly did not want to be chosen, and I could not be bothered with the ones who pursued me. At one point I realized that this might be a pathological problem, so I decided to see a therapist.

I went to a woman who came highly recommended by my friends. I poured out my story in the first session, summing up my history with the comment, "Anyway, I'm here because I want to have a real relationship and get married. But I think there's something in me that sabotages that."

She looked at me and said, "Well, I'm single and I'd like to get married too, so I don't think I can guarantee that. But I do think it's a pretty safe bet that you have a lot of difficult, painful work ahead of you."

I continued seeing her for several years and experienced, as fully as I was able to, the truth of that prediction. This also marked my discovery of the value of sitting in my brokenness. But my romantic encounters remained the same.

There is a river whose streams shall make
     glad the city of God,
The holy place of the tabernacle of the Most High.
     God is in the midst of her, she shall not be moved;
God shall help her, just at the break of dawn.

—PSALM 46:4–5, NKJV

Lord, all my desire is before You;
     and my sighing is not hidden from You.

—PSALM 38:9, NKJV

The sacrifices of God are a broken spirit,
     A broken and a contrite heart—
these, O God, You will not despise.

—PSALM 51:17, NKJV

In 1989, I finally had two relationships back-to-back, which supplied the inspiration for most of the songs on my first record. The record was called *Big Town,* and it was a catalog of hope and despair. The second relationship was with a man with whom I had absolutely nothing in common—except codependency. He had vague aspirations musically but no particular drive or giftedness; he was easy on the eyes but inside he was angry, mean, and, of course, unavailable. I was convinced that I loved him and signed on immediately as the driving force in what was at best an uneasy alliance. I managed to keep it alive for eight months—which constituted an all-time record for me. Convinced that we would marry, I was shattered when he finally ran.

I woke up crying one morning and had the sad epiphany that perhaps marriage and relationships with men in general were not in the cards for me. There was no relief or resolve in this conclusion; it just seemed obvious that I was incapable of anything but disastrous choices. Self-sufficiency and lack of trust in this area of my life had brought much suffering, not only for me but also for my little girl, and I couldn't continue to bring this kind of havoc into our world. I became willing to surrender.

But here's the deal about letting go: There's the day you decide to let go, and then there's the day you actually do it. They are, in my experience, rarely the same day.

I knew I was sitting on a powder keg of longing that played a powerful role in my choices and behavior. My bid for freedom seemed to demand letting it out, but I was afraid. I thought that expressing those feelings fully would kill me or, at the very least, confirm my worst fears about myself. But once again that is not what happened.

I began my odyssey of letting go by wearing a Band-Aid over my heart, outside my clothes, every day for more than a month. Everywhere I went, people would ask, "Why do you have that Band-Aid there?" or "Did you know you have a Band-Aid there?"

I always gave the same reply: "I have a broken heart." I know the teenage grocery store clerks viewed me as a poster child for pitiful losers, but I didn't care. I can remember driving around, sobbing uncontrollably, crying out to the Lord, "I just want to be picked!" I had spent so many years trying to convince men (including my father) of my value. The effort was overwhelming to me and I wanted very badly to be rid of it.

This went on for months—I felt as if I was constantly leaking—but finally I reached a place of peace, and I knew that I had accepted whatever my future held. I was not happy or particularly excited about it, and my desire to be deeply loved by a man was still very much intact. But I did believe that whatever the Lord had in mind for me, I could bear and bear well, without the crippling attempts to manage my longings.

I had also taken stock of the blessings He had poured out upon me, and I found many, many reasons to be grateful. On bad days I thought of all the rotten marriages I had witnessed over the years and was thankful not to be in one.

Unless the Lord builds the house,
they labor in vain who build it.

—PSALM 127:1, NKJV

Bless the Lord, O my soul;
And all that is within me, bless His holy name!
Bless the Lord, O my soul,
And forget not all His benefits:
Who forgives all your iniquities,
Who heals all your diseases,
Who redeems your life from destruction,
Who crowns you with lovingkindness and tender mercies,
Who satisfies your mouth with good things,
So that your youth is renewed like the eagle's.

—PSALM 103:1–5, NKJV

For He knows our frame;
He remembers that we are dust.

—PSALM 103:14, NKJV

On the surface, Kenny Greenberg looked like another reckless guitar gunslinger. I'd had a crush on him for years, but he was wrapped up pretty tight. That reserve, plus my admiration for his musical gifts, kept me from my usual pursuit. What I didn't know was that the Lord was stirring up a longing in him for something deeper and more lasting than anything he had ever experienced in a relationship with a woman. In 1989, I put together a band and asked Kenny if he would play guitar in it. Once we started playing together we began, very gradually, to be friends. We spent a lot of time working on *Big Town,* and I kept discovering things about him that drew me to him. Still, I never made a play. I was afraid of making a fool of myself and losing an ideal guitar player at the same time.

Then, over the course of a year, the friendship began to deepen and change. Our conversations became more revealing, and we discovered similar, life-changing experiences in our childhoods that added to the bond. One afternoon, when we were at a club doing sound checks, Kenny offered to take my seven-year-old daughter, Rebecca, to McDonald's. They walked out the door holding hands, and I teared up watching them, thinking for the first time in quite a while, *Lord, why can't Becca and I have this?*

Finally one night we went to see a movie and closed a restaurant talking afterward. Kenny came back to my house, and we continued talking, sitting up half the night. At one point he looked at me and said that we'd been friends for a long time but that his feelings for me had grown into something more. Our first kiss was the most passionate, tender, promising kiss I had ever had, and I knew, at last, that I had been picked.

*For (He satisfies the longing soul,
and fills the hungry soul with goodness.*

—PSALM 107:9, NKJV

We were married seven months later. Kenny adopted Rebecca and gave his heart to her as well as to me, and we now have two more children, Henry and Lily. This April we'll celebrate our tenth anniversary—pretty good for the girl with a short shelf life. It seems to me that God played to my weakness in this story. He certainly didn't wait for me to get it together to fulfill a desire of my heart; but even more fundamentally, He used my fear of rejection and loss to keep me from pursuing Kenny so that he could pursue me. He also used my penchant for unavailable men to attract me initially to a man who seemed to be just another bad idea but who proved to be faithful, devoted, and present. Best of all, the softness that came about as a result of letting my longings and sorrows surface was the very thing that Kenny said began to attract him to me romantically.

Of course, there are no fairy tales down here on earth; marriage is as much an opportunity to come to the end of yourself as it is for fulfillment, and we've had many very bad days. We are sinful, fragmented people, living in pieces, longing for the wholeness of heaven, and trying to content ourselves with tiny tastes between here and there.

But oh, how those tastes go a long, long way!

A SONG OF HOPE

Water

Water to a woman in the desert
Healing to the driest bones
I have longed for this; I have wept and prayed
Believing I would live to see this day
But faith gets lost along the way
To vows in sand and hearts of clay
Water

More than the sum of every petition
Better than the best laid plans
There is no guesswork here, no old wrongs to right
No creeping fears or notions of flight
Just a show of hands in the sweetest kiss
And a lifetime left for nights like this
Water

I'll be the watchman at your borders

Like the tattoos on your shoulder

I have made my peace, I could ask no more

I am signing off through this open door

I will take your name, I will wear your ring

And put aside every childish thing

Water

STRENGTH:
IN HIS GRASP

REBECCA ST. JAMES

I will sing of your might;
    I will sing aloud of your steadfast love
in the morning.
    For you have been a fortress for me
and a refuge in the day of my distress.
    O my strength,
I will sing praises to you.

—PSALM 59:16–17, NRSV

*I*t WAS A RACE I will never forget. It was the kind of event you didn't have to participate in to be moved and inspired by. In fact, you didn't even have to be there to "get it." The truth is that I watched the race from half a world away in the safety and comfort of our motor home on the road, months after the event actually took place.

Set in my homeland of Australia, this particular adventure caught my interest from the beginning. Known as the Eco-Challenge, this tax-your-body-to-the-limit quest is incredibly tough, to say the least. How does this sound—three hundred miles of nonstop kayaking, hiking, mountain biking, cliff climbing, walking, and rafting? It's exhausting to even think of! The race takes seven to ten days, with teams stopping only for the rest needed to survive. Organizers say that the key ingredients in this race are honest communication, compassion, and remaining mission-oriented. Part of the goal of Eco-Challengers is simply to finish the race, as some do not.

With contestants coming from all around the world, obviously I was rooting for my home team to win. But it was not the Australians or their courage that impacted me so greatly. It was a Chinese team, three guys and a girl, who inspired me so much that I wrote a song about them (included at the end of this chapter). Here's the story.

The race had begun, and the Chinese team was progressing through the rough Australian land. Then the nightmare began. It became clear that the lone female member was in pain—one foot began to weaken notice-ably. Still she kept on. Finally, after many miles, she could go no farther. She could not put weight on her foot, let alone hike the distance still remaining. It was a disaster, and the Chinese team was looking at the very real possibility of not finishing the race.

One of the most important rules in the Eco-Challenge is that all team members must cross the finish line together. So do you know what they did? Instead of quitting, seeing this misfortune as the end, they found another way to keep on with the race. The strong loaned their strength to the weak. The men in the team took turns running ahead and resting so that when the team caught up, a "rested" member could take the woman from the back of his teammate and carry her. To see their commitment to finish together and not give up brought tears to my eyes. They even had to pack her up mountains, help her over rocks, and carry her through the forest. It was so inspiring!

To me their story is such a vivid picture of what the true Christian family should look like. It is a reminder of what Christian brotherhood and sisterhood is all about. We must love our brothers and sisters in the Lord so much that we would help them cross the finish line even at great cost to ourselves. Jesus said there is no greater love than when a man lays down his life for his friends (John 15:13). I truly believe that God often uses you and me to help give His strength to other members of the body. We are to carry each other's burdens—but ultimately it is God who carries us.

God is our refuge and strength,
a very present help in trouble.
Therefore we will not fear.

—PSALM 46:1–2, NRSV

I really began to sense God carrying me when I began singing professionally. I remember well my first time on stage alone. I was thirteen years old and opening for Carman on his Revival in the Land tour. I'd practiced for months beforehand but still felt some pretty serious nerves prior to going out there to do the real thing. I remember joining hands and praying with Carman and other members of his group, asking that God's Spirit and strength would be with us. That first night I began a tradition that for seven years now has enabled me to do what I do. Without God's power and His Spirit, I know that all my efforts are useless. It is only God who changes lives, and knowing that frees me to simply delight in serving Him. Then I get to sit back and watch what He does. The pressure is not on me, and I can rest in the fact that I am not in control—He is!

Since that first night there have been so many other experiences where my faith has been tested and deepened. When my family first moved to America in 1991, we went through a major living-by-faith experience. We moved from Australia to Nashville, Tennessee, because of my dad's job. About two months after coming to America, my dad's job fell through. We were left on the other side of the world with no family, no close friends, no car, no furniture, no income, six kids, and my mum pregnant with the seventh. To say my parents were at a loss and rather humbled would be an incredible understatement. We didn't know what God was doing or even why we were in America. My grandparents even called us from Australia and begged us to come home.

What did we do? We sat on the floor as a family and prayed. We asked God for money, for food—for a car. We prayed specifically for God to provide the things we needed, and we saw miracles happen! Sometimes those specific things would come the same day we prayed for them. People dropped groceries on our doorstep, sent us checks in the mail, delivered truckloads of furniture to our house—somebody even gave us a Christmas tree and presents that first year! One family gave us a car. Someone paid thousands of dollars for my sister Libby to be born in a hospital; to this day we still don't know who that was!

Because of these experiences and others, I know that even when it feels as if life is at its worst and I've come to a dead end in the strength department, somehow God will surprise me with modern-day miracles. It may be as simple as someone saying an encouraging word at the right time or God revealing a Bible verse just for me, right when I need it. Or it may be that He places on my doorstep a houseful of furniture!

Truly, if we are His children and are trusting Him to take care of us—He will! Often when we're going through a hard time, it's not going to feel good in the fire, but God's promise stands that He will be with us.

Once when I was going through a hard time, I asked my pastor about how to deal with pain. He asked me, "Can God be trusted?"

"Yes," I answered.

I got the point: He's trustworthy, so trust Him. When I am weak, He is strong.

God is my help;
the Lord is the one who sustains me.

—PSALM 54:4

I love you, O Lord, my strength.
The Lord is my rock,
my fortress, and my deliverer,
my God, my rock in whom I take refuge.

—PSALM 18:1–2, NRSV

There is another thought that keeps me going in hard times. It is the moment I reach heaven and my eyes meet Jesus' eyes for the first time. I look forward to it so much. He looks at me and our eyes lock. And then there it is, that instant of recognition: "I know You and You know me. I've spent my life speaking to You, loving You, listening to You, reading about You, knowing You, and now I see You!" It will be the most amazing feeling I will ever know.

This vision of Jesus gives me strength for the journey, helps me dance through life and not just trudge through it. When I weaken in the race, He lifts me to His back and carries me. He is my joy, and the joy that He brings is my strength.

✣

A SONG OF STRENGTH

I'll Carry You

I know that look in your eyes; I see the pain behind your smile
Please don't hold it all inside
Together we can run to the finish line
And when you are tired—I'll carry you

I can't walk this road without you
You cannot go it alone
We were never meant to make it on our own
When the load becomes too heavy
And your feet too tired to walk
I will carry you
And we'll be carried on

Share your burden now—I will listen
And when I'm weak will you hold me to the truth?
That we can go on for we are carried
Three strands of cord cannot be easily torn

I can't walk this road without you

You cannot go it alone

We were never meant to make it on our own

When the load becomes to heavy

And your feet too tired to walk

I will carry you

And we'll be carried on

God will carry us, God will carry us

Before I say one more word

Hear me say, "I Love You"

My love comes from a heart that overflows

With love who fills me

Comforts me, comforts you

With arms stretched out He said, "I'll Carry You"

PeRSpECTIVe RESTORed

KIM HILL
with LISA HARPER

If the Lord delights in a man's way,
*   he makes his steps firm;*
though he stumble,
*   he will not fall,*
for the Lord upholds him with his hand.

—PSALM 37:23–24

I WAS DIGGING AROUND for some papers the other day and came upon the buried treasure of my elementary school yearbooks. I turned the pages slowly, smiling at pictures that flooded my mind with nostalgic memories about the small town in Mississippi where I grew up. Then I found my seventh-grade class picture, a grinning eleven-year-old face complete with pigtails and Coke-bottle glasses. One especially creative classmate had written in the margin next to my photo, "To a nice, flat-chested, four-eyed girl!"

My chest is fine, thank you very much, but my eyes got worse every year. By the time I was in high school, I could barely make out the big E without glasses. Fortunately, Mom understood the complex social pressures of a teenager and let me get contact lenses. And for more than twenty years I followed the morning ritual of waking up unable to see the two-inch neon numbers on the bedside clock, feeling around clumsily for my glasses (often knocking over a half-full water glass in the process), biting back bad words because of the water on the carpet, stumbling to the bathroom, fumbling for my contact case, then squirting, poking, and blinking until—Ta-da! I could see!

Aside from spilling drinks and stubbing my toes on the bed frame, I didn't really consider my morning routine a negative. Contacts were my ticket to 20/20 vision; the alternative—wearing glasses the thickness of a

Big Mac—was so much worse. But I would've gladly doused myself with freezing water and whacked my toes every morning if it meant being able to see clearly.

Then I had Lasik surgery (with an angel masquerading as a doctor named Dale), which miraculously healed my wimpy retinas. Within twenty-four hours I could see perfectly with my eyes in all their naked glory—no glasses or contacts! The first morning after the surgery, I woke up and watched the numbers change on the clock. I couldn't believe I could actually see what time it was. The best thing was watching my two-year-old son's face change expressions from delight to earnest appeal for powdered doughnuts a few minutes later. Watching the subtle movements in his sweet face while I was still in bed was a first-time treasure. I just wanted to lie there and watch him and let him eat doughnuts until dinner!

It's been well over a year since my eye surgery, and I'm still amazed that I can see—that I don't have to poke a plastic disk in my eye before I can see the clock, read Benji's face or Martha's magazine, or drive car pool. I have to rein myself in to keep from handing out my eye doctor's card to everyone wearing glasses in the mall or the grocery store!

If only perfect spiritual eyesight were as simple as a fifteen-minute outpatient procedure. When it comes to God's will and timing, my vision can get pretty blurry. Sometimes, when the circumstances in my life look bleak, His faithfulness is shrouded by a veil of doubt. I stumble around in the darkness and wonder if He sees me. And if He does, does He really care about me? Does He know what I'm walking through? Was this trial supposed to last this long? Has He forgotten me?

[Journal entry] Whenever I read about the Prodigal Son, I'm overwhelmed that God loves me like that—that He hugs me, kisses me, holds me when I come home to Him after wandering off. That He says, "Return to Me, Kim, for I have redeemed you"—that He loves me. That when He sprinkles clean water on me, I am clean. "They will walk with me, dressed in white, for they are worthy" (Revelation 3:4). *If I confess my sin, He is so faithful and just to forgive me, to cleanse me from all unrighteousness.*

When I'm blinded by discouragement and asking all kinds of questions, I've often made the mistake of running to whoever will listen to me. One day after a particularly awful fight with my husband, I called my mom and poured out my anger and frustration. She listened for a while and then finally said, "Kim, I've got to go. You're wearing me out! Your life is too much for me to handle right now."

My mother is one of the best listeners in the world. She has given me wonderful, godly counsel over and over again. But on that day she just couldn't take my complaints anymore. I remember hanging up the phone in stunned disbelief. I couldn't believe my own mother was tired of listening to me!

Then, almost as clear as my mom's voice had been on the phone, the Lord whispered to me. He reminded me that He is the one I'm supposed to run to in times of trouble and distress. He is the only one able to handle the emotional acidity of my pain and disillusionment. He is the only one able to give me unrelenting peace along with renewed hope and perspective. I've wasted so much time and energy running to other things—to other people—for relief. He is right there—He just asks me to seek Him.

I love the old hymn that says it best: "Turn your eyes upon Jesus, look full in His wonderful face; and the things of earth will grow strangely dim in the light of His glory and grace."

[Journal entry] Have mercy on me, O God. Open my eyes and ears to Your Holy Spirit so that I may be comforted by Your perfect peace. Please forgive me for doubting Your plans for my life. Teach me to trust in Your sovereignty. Help me to rest in Your goodness. I want to understand Your ways, Lord. Quiet my restless heart, and hold me next to Your everlasting breast.

It is during my intimate moments alone with Him in prayer that God performs delicate surgery on the cataracts covering my soul. He gently removes my doubt and fear and uncovers the faith He breathed into my life when I was a little girl. He reminds me that He is always faithful and that His plans for me are perfect, regardless of what today looks like. He's teaching me to stop and listen for His voice first when I can't see around the corner of my circumstances. And His voice is unmistakable in His Word.

Lord, You know me inside and out,
Better than I know myself.
You know me when I'm sleeping
And when I'm running around.
You know even my thoughts.
You see everywhere I go and
What I do when no one is looking.
Before I even say a word,
You know what it is going to be.
With Your strong right hand,
You protect me from every angle.
I can't understand all of this —
Your ways are so much higher than mine.
I can't go anywhere to escape from
Your Spirit or Your sight,

Because even darkness is as bright as the day to You.
Look inside my heart and mind
And know what I'm worried about—
Where I'm doubting You.
Help me walk in the right way
And lead me on Your perfect path.

(MY INTERPRETATION OF PSALM 139:1–10, 23–24)

More often than not, the obstacle or "offensive way" that keeps me in high weeds instead of on His perfect path is my own pride: the ludicrous notion that I can find the way by myself. Just like some bearded guy in a truck with gun racks, I pretend that I don't need any help with directions.

When I was in college at Mississippi State University, I didn't own a pair of glasses because I was too embarrassed to wear them even when I needed to. The girls in the dorm used to laugh and call me Helen Keller because I literally "felt" my way down the hall to the bathroom after I had taken my contacts out.

Late one night, I ran my hands down the sides of the walls—by then very familiar to me—made my way to the rest room, and sat down. The dorm was quiet, and I sat there, relieved to have made it safely in the dark. But then I looked up and saw the giant blurred shape of a man looming above me. I screamed for help at the top of my lungs, bracing myself for the anonymous stranger's attack. But then I realized that he was screaming too. I had scared one of our star football players half to death! Talk about falling off the throne—Mr. Mitchell was using our bathroom for a midnight rendezvous with his girlfriend and didn't expect to be discovered by a half-blind coed!

In the same way my vanity kept me from wearing glasses in college, my pride sometimes keeps me from seeking God's direction now. Just as I stubbornly groped down the walls of Rice Hall, I still stumble along groping for clues. Instead of running to the Creator of the universe, I run blindly into obstacles on paths He didn't choose for me. And some of my collisions hurt a lot worse than a stubbed toe.

But God is never surprised by my faithless floundering. He isn't shocked by my bumbling spiritual blindness. Just as I know that my two boys will experience bumps and bruises when they don't listen to my instructions, how much more my heavenly Father understands my rebellious rambling.

Keep me alive,
    so I can praise you,
and let me find help
    in your teachings.

I am your servant,
but I have wandered away
like a lost sheep.
Please come after me,
because I have not forgotten
your teachings.

—PSALM 119:175–176, CEV

In his every-Christian-must-read book *Knowing God,* J. I. Packer wrote, "Wisdom is the power to see, and the inclination to choose the best and highest goal, together with the surest means of attaining it."[1] God is the only one who is capable of possessing perfect wisdom. He is the only one who can see, choose, and attain the best for my life—because He can see around the corners of my life.

I must admit that I've doubted if He was actually choosing the best for me during the last few years. Some days I feel as if I've been crammed into a vise of hurt that won't stop squeezing. I've been overwhelmed with decisions about which way to run and when to stop running. I've spent hours on the floor in my office, begging for divine direction. I've never been so completely "blind" in my whole life. Quite frankly, sometimes my perspective has been limited to daily survival.

[Journal entry] Joseph actually told his brothers not to feel bad for what they had done to him, that God planned it so He could save them. Can I say that to Rob (my ex-husband) when he hurts me? Can I believe that this is all worth it for me to be closer to the Lord— more desperate for Him?

"Before they call, I will answer; And while they are still speaking, I will hear" (Isaiah 65:24, NKJV).

Yet God hears my cries. Just when I think I can't take another step, He lifts my head and gives me hope. Throughout this season of not seeing, God has graciously given me Damascus mornings—moments of perfect vision and clarity when He reminds me of His amazing grace. Sometimes He even turns my mourning into dancing, and I wiggle while worshiping alone in my office. I'm beginning to understand that most of my "obstacles" are heaven-sent because they bring me to my knees and to His merciful throne.

Though I can't quite wrap my mind around God's omniscience, I can choose to respond in faith to the inscrutability of God's wisdom, power, and plans for my life. When the drama of my life doesn't necessarily point to a loving God, I can take my thoughts captive and remember that His providence is perfect. When the twists and turns I'm navigating don't make sense, His Spirit changes my perspective to see that His ways are above my ways as the heavens are above the earth. When I can't see light at the end of the tunnel, that is when I truly learn that He is El Roi—the God who sees everything.

I cry aloud to the Lord;
        I lift up my voice to the Lord for mercy.
I pour out my complaint before him;
        before him I tell my trouble.
When my spirit grows faint within me,
        it is you who know my way.

—PSALM 142:1–3

[Journal entry] Lord,…I want to hear Your voice more clearly…to have my perspective ordered by Your Spirit. Guide me Father…please be my vision.

1. J. I. Packer, *Knowing God* (Downers Grove, Ill.: InterVarsity Press, 1973).

A SONG OF RESTORATION
I Can't Believe

I can't believe that You would love me
When I have walked away from You
I can't believe that You would trust me
After all I've put You through

I never thought that I could be so close to You
I never thought it could be this way
But now I know, it's all I know
It is my dream that You would love me so

I can't believe that You could find me
When I had wandered off so far
I can't believe that You would claim me
When I acted like I don't know who You are

I never thought that I could be so close to You

I never thought it could be this way

But now I know, it's all I know

It is my dream that You would love me so

To stand before You at the throne of grace

To feel You wipe my tears away

To lay at Your feet like a blameless child

And hear You whisper, gently whisper my name

Now I know, it's all I know

It is my dream that You would love me so.

Trust

NICHOLE NORDEMAN

*My eyes are ever toward the Lord,
for he will pluck my feet out of the net.*

—PSALM 25:15, NRSV

I HAVE TYPICALLY BEEN someone who approaches her spiritual life in the same way I approached finals week in college: with lots of procrastinating, many good and honest intentions, plenty of lofty goals—but never cracking a book until the night before the big test. And while this may have worked for my physics class, it is not exactly an effective or mature way to attain new spiritual insight or growth.

That said, to meet my deadline for this book, I have been forced (gratefully) to actually sit down with my Bible and my thoughts so I could jot down some of my own musings regarding the Psalms. It was the first time in a while that I took the time to listen to the voice of God. And the funniest thing happened: I actually heard Him. And I've wondered several times since then how different my faith journey would be if I engaged in some "scheduled reflection" a little more often—instead of waiting for my life to spontaneously make room for God's presence, which it never does.

One of my discoveries was this: God's plans can be so unnerving. The psalmists reaffirm this truth often! Now, when I refer to "God's plans," I'm pretty sure that's what they are, although I can never say for sure the way some people can. To tell you the truth, I've never felt especially comfortable talking about God's activities or God's will because it sounds so presumptuous. How does one actually "know" what God is up to? How could we? And yet I'm stunned at the number of people who talk as if God accidentally left His Palm Pilot in the back of a cab, and after picking it up, they now have detailed information regarding God's plans for their lives. It just sounds a little dangerous to me. When we begin to casually stamp God's seal of approval on our own agendas ("God told me this" or "God told me that"), we run the risk of confusing our own desires with His plans.

For example, I know people who are very solid, salt-of-the-earth, dig-your-heels-in kind of Christians who attribute everything that happens in their lives to God's providential hand. And not just miraculous healings, either—everything from an unexpected, prime parking space in a crowded parking lot to a sale on avocados just in time for the taco salad they were hoping to make for dinner. All of these things, they would tell you, are direct evidence of God's goodness and involvement in their lives. In fact, God's actual intimate involvement in our day-to-day activity has become a new buzz phrase that I'm sure you've heard many times: "It's a God thing." I think we use this expression because somehow, as Christians, we feel it is inappropriate to use words like *coincidence* and *irony,* so instead we take the credit upstairs. When in doubt we state, "It must be a God thing."

My friends who are not Christians have their own lingo for the same miraculous healing/parking space/avocado sale moments. They usually offer phrases such as, "Hey, everything happens for a reason" and "You must have been in the right place at the right time." And while those sound a bit too New Age for my own theological taste, I'm not sure they are any more ridiculous than the assumption that God ordained your taco salad.

I think I land somewhere in the middle. I believe to my core that God moves very deliberately and carefully in the details of our lives. Jesus said so when He told us that even sparrows and lilies are beneficiaries of the Father's love and deep concern. So it stands to reason that He would care even more deeply for us. But in my humanity there are moments when I'm still hesitant to credit the Creator of the universe with the small stuff, not because He couldn't or wouldn't care about the intricate moments in my life, but because the ten o'clock news tells me there's still no peace in the Middle East, and so I imagine He must be pretty tied up at the moment. So I resort to a fairly hurried prayer life, an occasional glance at Scripture, and a host of skeptical responses to the many people I meet who hear the voice of God with much more clarity than I ever have.

Frankly, my frustrated attempts at hearing God's voice can make life difficult at times. It's just plain hard to trust in someone who at once seems so big, so vast, and so removed from our silly little lives.

Yet another discovery I made while contemplating the psalmists' words recently speaks to this. It was the sense of kinship I felt when I read their poetry. People are drawn to the Psalms for different reasons, I think. Many feel led to specific passages that speak of God's goodness and steadfastness; others invoke Psalms as a way of expressing joyful worship and praise; but I think I'm drawn to David's words of struggle because they validate my own struggles somehow. There are so many "Where are You?" Psalms that I wonder if, like myself, David didn't also have a hard time hearing the voice of God and trusting in a divine hope and future. He wrote:

Be gracious to me, O God,
    for people trample on me;
all day long foes oppress me;
        my enemies trample on me all day long,
for many fight against me.
    O Most High, when I am afraid,
I put my trust in you.

—PSALM 56:1–3, NRSV

When I read this type of passage, I always picture David crouched behind some rock, fearing for his life and breathing this kind of prayer quietly as he narrowly escapes the watchful eye of his enemy. I generally do not share this type of experience. My enemies are usually not flesh and blood and armed with crude, prehistoric weapons. And I can't remember the last time I felt oppressed or trampled by my foes all day long. But I do understand David's prayer and the desire of his heart to learn how to trust in his God without hesitation.

In another passage, he wrote:

I lift up my eyes to the hills—
from where will my help come?
My help comes from the Lord,
who made heaven and earth.

—PSALM 121:1–2, NRSV

Again, in my mind I see a very literal picture of David fearing for his safety, glancing frantically up into the hills for a place of sanctuary and peace, even if just for a few moments. And again, while I do not often fear for my life, I have certainly "lifted my eyes" to plenty of my own hills, hoping for a reprieve, a momentary pardon from my own enemies. My enemies are those of time and obligation and the pressure that comes from expectations set far too high. Like David, I am forced to trust in an unseen hand to cover me from harm, to move me out of dark places, and to keep me in the places that are necessary, no matter how uncomfortable, for my growth.

The ability to trust God—*really* trust Him—remains a great challenge for me. Truth be told, I've become quite skilled at trusting Him selectively. Handing over the small stuff is not a problem. Letting go of the big things is a different story. Sometimes my struggle to trust God reminds me of my parents' approach to my first days as a licensed, adolescent driver behind the wheel of my first car. I had imagined that my life would change on my sixteenth birthday, that I would finally have an all-access pass to the world. In reality, it resembled something like probation. I was allowed to drive up to the corner market, but only during the daytime. I could drive with other friends, but only if they were on the "approved friend" list. I could drive to and from school, and occasionally to church, but never out to the movies on a Friday night.

Simply put, my parents didn't trust me. This was maddening, and I can recall more than one door-slamming fight with my dad (I slammed, he didn't) where I would beg and plead and cry, "This isn't freedom!" I wanted carte blanche—my own wheels, my own plan.

This is the conversation I have with God sometimes: "God, You can drive my life up to the corner market and back but only during the day…"

And He cries, "This isn't freedom!" He desires carte blanche as well, only unlike the inexperienced sixteen-year-old driver, He deserves it. He requires it.

Maybe it's a "God thing," but when I started to read the Psalms, specifically the ones that dealt with the issue of trust, and write down my own struggles in that area, I began to see with new eyes opportunities to trust God with the big stuff. Everyone I know faces many crossroads at which to trust—or not.

For example, I just helped move my grandparents out of their house of twenty years into a smaller, more manageable townhouse in a different city so that my mom can better care for them during the last seasons of their lives. They are understandably very nervous about the whole process and have had a difficult time trusting us (and God) that this is the right thing. My grandfather, a brilliant man and former fighter pilot, now cannot remember whether or not he had lunch a few hours ago. And it's very frightening for him to admit that he must now be dependent on someone else for even the smallest thing. Like David, he must learn to lift up his eyes to the hills.

A good friend just e-mailed me with the news that his company is unexpectedly shutting its doors and he will be forced to find work elsewhere. He has many mouths to feed at home and is confident in the Lord, but he is still apprehensive about what's next. And so he lifts up his eyes to the hills.

My best friend, Amy, an exceptionally gifted vocalist and actress, just moved back to New York last week with her dream of finally getting her break on Broadway. She has very limited resources with which to finance this dream. But she lifts up her eyes to the hills.

And as for me, I have been engaged to be married now for about a month. And along with the inexplicable and overwhelming gratitude I feel for the gift God has given me in a man who loves me with a love that only God could have imagined, I also have a healthy fear of what marriage will bring. Will I be the kind of partner my spouse needs? Will I learn to give from a place of selflessness and not just reciprocation? What if I'm not so great at marriage?

I, too, must lift up my eyes to the hills and trust that the same God who delivered David from his enemies and gave him reason to dance and sing can be trusted with my life. And having taken the time to hear His voice again, I am confident that He can drive past the corner market. At night, even.

A SONG OF TRUST

Small Enough

Oh, great God, be small enough to hear me now.
There were times when I was crying from the dark of Daniel's den
And I have asked You once or twice if You would part the sea again
But tonight I do not need a fiery pillar in the sky
Just want to know You're gonna hold me if I start to cry
Oh, great God, be close enough to feel You now

Oh, great God, be close enough to feel You now
There have been moments when I could not face Goliath on my own
How could I forget we've marched around our share of Jerichos
But I will not be setting out a fleece for You tonight
Just want to know that everything will be all right
Oh, great God, be close enough to feel You now

All praise and all the honor be

To the God of ancient mysteries

Whose every sign and wonder turn the pages of our history

But tonight my heart is heavy

And I cannot keep from whispering this prayer,

"Are You there?"

And I know You could leave writing on the wall that's just for me

Or send wisdom while I'm sleeping, like in Solomon's sweet dreams

But I don't need the strength of Samson, or a chariot in the end

Just want to know that You still know how many hairs are on my head

Oh, great God,

Be small enough to hear me now

By Nichole Nordeman. © 2000 Ariose Music/Admin.
by EMI Christian Music Publishing/(ASCAP).
All rights reserved. Used by permission.

THANKSGIVING OFFERED

MARGARET BECKER

Enter his gates with thanksgiving
and his courts with praise;
give thanks to him and praise his name.
For the Lord is good and
his love endures forever;
his faithfulness continues through all
generations.

—PSALM 100:4–5

I was stuck in Denver rush-hour traffic with my band one hot summer afternoon. Jammed into an old van, U-Haul trailer in tow, we idled silently in the sea of cars. Every ten minutes or so, we moved forward a few feet as I nervously watched the temperature gauge lean farther and farther into the red. We'd already turned on the heater to compensate, and we all had a sheen of sweat to bear witness.

We were miserable and late, of all things. We were due more than an hour earlier at a sound check. As each moment passed, the dashboard's digital clock became a chafing reminder of our situation.

We'd traveled six miles in an hour when the traffic finally began to free up. With less than one hour to get to the venue, set up, sound check, eat, and shower, the race was on. Dave floored it. We all fell back into our seats, relieved.

Seconds later we crested a hill and I watched as Dave stood almost upright in his seat, jamming down on the brake. Directly in front of us lay three lanes of immovable metal and rubber: traffic at a dead stop.

The van shuddered and began to sway as the trailer wagged lazily. Smoke from the burning brakes trailed behind us, and the expletives flew as we braced for impact. Clutching the back of Dave's seat, I leaned forward for a better view. From the moment the braking began, I went into a default mode, which in this case was instruction, encouragement, and thanks: "You're doing great, Dave, just keep us straight. *Thank You, Jesus.* That's it, you can do it. *Thank You, Jesus.*" Toward the last few moments, my thank-you mantra accelerated until it was comprised of only *"Thank You, Jesus, thank You, Jesus, thank You, Jesus"* spoken at warp speed, the way only a New Yorker can.

As we hurtled the last few car lengths, Dave miraculously guided the van to the left shoulder, narrowly missing the small Toyota in front of us. We came to a halt, trailer slightly askew, but all told, very much intact.

Troy, my bass player, sat white faced and breathless. *"Yes,* thank You, *Jesus!"* he rasped. Turning to me, he penitently offered, "I'm sorry I cussed."

"Man, Dave! I don't know how you did it!" Jeff, my drummer, said as he playfully mussed Dave's hair.

"That could have been very serious," Tim, the guitarist, added.

Exhausted, Dave whined, "Why couldn't it have been any of you in this seat? I only weigh a hundred pounds and I couldn't jam the brakes hard enough!"

Laughter erupted, and Tim turned to me and said, "And then there was Margaret and her 'Thank You, Jesus, thank You, Jesus, thank You, Jesus!' Why would you be thanking God for a car wreck?"

"Hey," I offered, "I figure if I am going to meet Him, I don't want the last words on my lips to be something I have to repent for!"

As we pulled back into traffic, the words *Thank You, Jesus* rose up in the van like a rap classic, sung in the best Margaret Becker imitation that grown men could muster. It became known as the "Thank You, Jesus" song, and before that tour was through, we'd all sung it many times.

You see, early on in my pursuit of Jesus, I'd learned a difficult principle: God knows all things, and although not all things are what He would desire for us, all things are ultimately under His power—both the good and the bad. I truly don't understand the cause-and-effect relationship of faith entirely; I just know that God sees, and He knows it all before it even transpires. So in some way, in even the most tragic and terrible of circumstances, His presence permeates, and the age-old promise that He will make "all things work together for the good" comes to bear.

If that is true, then ultimately His will will be accomplished, His kingdom will be glorified, and we will have had the opportunity to be a part of that process, which is the highest honor of all. My response to that honor is thanks, as Scripture exhorts, "In everything give thanks" (1 Thessalonians 5:18, NASB). I take it to heart and I thank God for all things, all day long (when I remember to do it, which is an art form in itself—remembering, that is).

I thank because I believe that it pleases God to hear my tiny voice lifting off His vast earth, offering simple words of gratitude in response to His intricate acts of mercy.

I thank because it reminds me of my ultimate truth: I am His. He is mine. All blessings flow from Him. All troubles ultimately conform me more to His image, and that is the highest aim of life. It's happening to me every day of my life. He is faithful to do it. It is cause to thank.

I thank because it reminds me of how fortunate I am. From the seemingly small details to the impossibly big ones, God expresses Himself continually in my life. Each expression is imbued with His postscript: I love you. My response to that love is to echo the psalmist:

Bless the Lord, O my soul;
And all that is within me, bless His holy name.
Bless the Lord, O my soul,
And forget none of His benefits.

—PSALM 103:1–2, NASB

I love the tone of that Psalm. It's bossy. It commands that ruling part of us all, the soul, the part that exerts its power apart from reasoning and will, to bless the Lord and forget not His gifts.

The soul, the center of our lives: It is the apex of our existence, powerful and eternal. It is not infallible, though; the soul can become distracted just like all the other parts of us. This Psalm demonstrates that the soul needs to be reminded of its source, its origination and destination, and its merciful Creator unseen—the Lord. And it needs to be reminded not only of His existence, but also that it should respond to Him with blessings, the simplest of which is thanks.

Thanks brings Him honor and brings us remembrance. It's a gift that is useful and beautiful to both parties, the giver and the receiver.

It is an act of reduction, for in thanking someone you are humbling yourself by acknowledging that power was exerted over you and it was pleasant.

It is an indication of trust. When you thank, the truth is that you gave the Recipient of the thanks entrance into your life and allowed Him close enough to affect you. That takes trust.

I give thanks for the peace thanksgiving brings. I always desire peace. I have a never-ending need of it, in fact. That is why thanksgiving is one of my most frequent forms of formal and informal communication with my God.

The Lord gives strength to his people;
the Lord blesses his people with peace.

—PSALM 29:11

One of the fundamental disciplines I have attempted to cultivate in my life is the practice of peace: the art of retreating inward, no matter what the outward experience, and settling my soul. It's a difficult undertaking at best. Daily barrages of tasks and stimuli see to that.

But in truth, no matter what the circumstance, our minds continually retreat somewhere while we carry on in the outward world. Some minds retreat to anxiety, tugging on the edges of malady, fraught with the belief that the very act of worry will somehow count toward solution. Some come to rest on a favorite memory or a future hope. And some find countless other places to frequent that are limited only by imagination.

My own propensities span the gamut, and frankly, I tire of my running to and fro seeking peace. Instead I try to take a cue from Philippians 4:6, which recommends three intertwined actions: prayer, supplication, and thanksgiving. When I retreat, I seek an inner place of communion, which I consider to be an ongoing dialogue with God.

We each have our own personal style with God. Mine is unique to me, and part of it involves not being a "Gimme." That's a term my parents would use for children who had everything they needed but never seemed to be satisfied.

I know that prayers are not always selfish, but the principle my parents taught through the "Gimmes" was thankfulness. They urged us to be grateful for all we had and to focus on all that was right. It was a lesson that stayed with me, and today my intercessions reflect it. Though my prayers cycle regularly to cover a multitude of concerns both global and personal, supplication is not my most frequent communication with God. Thanks is.

Like the psalmist, I believe this firmly:

It is good to give thanks to the Lord,
And to sing praises to Thy name, O Most High.

—PSALM 92:1, NASB

It *is* good—good, wonderful, helpful, reasonable, just, correct. It is, in fact, the very least that we should do and the very best of what we can do. But it is still a struggle for me, especially when the speeding car does not narrowly miss the one in front of it, and the sighs of relief are replaced with the sadness of a ripping heart. Oh, how frightening it is to give thanks in those moments, how difficult and symbolic the command to "bless the Lord" becomes at those turbulent times.

To thank Him in the midst of cancer? To bless Him in death? To praise Him in protracted suffering? Who can begin to even consider that kind of praise? And yet the practice of thanks—even the most tenuous of attempts—is the tiny thread of light that leads us out and weaves us into the ultimate tapestry of beauty, the character of Christ.

The patience, the humility, the hard task of holding on for dear life and finding peace along the way—all are tiny deaths in a sense: death of will, death of self, death of rigid expectation. They birth us into His form. They serve to remind us that we are mere and simple, small and insignificant, yet highly valued and noted by God, as the psalmist proclaims:

The cords of death entangled me,
the anguish of the grave came upon me;
I was overcome by trouble and sorrow.
Then I called on the name of the Lord:
"O Lord, save me!"
The Lord is gracious and righteous;

our God is full of compassion.
        The Lord protects the simplehearted;
when I was in great need, he saved me.
        Be at rest once more, O my soul,
for the Lord has been good to you.
        For you, O Lord, have delivered my soul from death,
my eyes from tears,
        my feet from stumbling,
that I may walk before the Lord
        in the land of the living.
Precious in the sight of the Lord
        is the death of his saints.
O Lord, truly I am your servant;
        I am your servant, the son of your maidservant;
you have freed me from my chains.
        I will sacrifice a thank offering to you.

—PSALM 116:3–8, 15–17

Even in the many deaths we endure both inside and outside ourselves, something spectacular happens: He accomplishes His will because the suffering serves to shape Christ in us and around us, and we exalt His kingdom.

This is a glorious honor. And when I've experienced it in this challenging form, the "Gimme" in me has risen up for a most noble task: "Please give me strength to bring You thanks through all this."

My simplistic take on this act of thanks is that it is a high form of praise and that it is truly the most profound gift I can offer while on this earth. I am certain even as the words tumble from my soul that they are not even touching the seams of "enough," but I see this moment by moment retreat as my continual, reasonable service of worship (Romans 12:1). It is my frankincense and myrrh. It is my fine oil poured out before the Lord. It is my mite. It is the inward bow of submission I make all throughout the day, acknowledging His glory. It is all I hope to do for eternity.

✛

A SONG OF THANKS

Who Am I

Who am I, Jesus
That You call me by name

I am counting the stars
On Your blackened sky
You call them all by name; You know them all by sight
In this sea of lights
I sense Your majesty
And I break at the thought that One so great
Could care for me

Who am I, Jesus
That You call me by name
What could I ever do
To be loved this way
Who am I, Jesus
In Your eyes, tell me who am I

I am counting the mountains

That I've laid at your feet

And I'm reduced to tears when I think of how

      You've moved them for me

In this storm of life

You've been my safe retreat

Through the wind and the fire You always were there

To carry me

Who am I, Jesus

That You call me by name

What could I ever do

To be loved this way

Who am I, Jesus

In Your eyes, tell me who am I

No greater honor could I ever find

Than the privilege to love You for the rest of my life

Who am I, Jesus

That You call me by name

What could I ever do

To be loved this way

Who am I, Jesus

In Your eyes, tell me who am I

Multnomah Publishers

The publisher and author would love to hear your
comments about this book. *Please contact us at:*
www.multnomah.net/danceofheaven